THE REBEL SUTRA

RAUNAK BARAL

Contents

Contents

Preface

This book comes out of my heart, after I had been challenged, as a poet. Over the course of my last two books, I feel, I have been growing as an author. I started out with my first book, The Ballads of Bengal, which dealt with mostly broken hearted pieces, with a touch of the dark side.

Having come out of the dark, and well into the light, I published An Ode to Boyhood Love, which spoke about a young man falling in love, a healthy love, for the first time, although unrequited. My third book, Kiran, too was a testimony to my love for my muse. It was only with my fourth book that I truly began speaking about deeper themes and spirituality.

I have been practicing Buddhism for over a decade now. And it has greatly shaped my ideas, visions and life, in general. I follow these principles that I have learnt and recognized over time, realizing their essence, and internalizing them, as I grew and evolved as an individual.

The book of poetry, The Rebel Sutra, is born from my deep love of this Buddhist Philosophy (Nichiren Daishonin's Buddhism),and it speaks of my realizations, obstacles, and lessons as I passed my 35th year and entered my 36th.

Although I may have spoken about love, as an offchance, that is not the mainstay of this book. The purpose of this book is to educate and illuminate. Concepts that often feel unreachable for the average person — I've attempted to simplify and illuminate them through verse, which human beings are so familiar to!

I have spoken about spirituality in a way that can be comprehended. For many of us, we are in doubt regarding to what spirituality means for us. To be really simple, it is accepting ourselves as we are, learning about how our minds and hearts operate, and trying to get a connection with the Divine and the rest of the world. It is in connecting with our environments and following a certain path that we feel will lead to our highest good.

It is not in uttering mumbo-jumbo, or great rituals. It is in honouring the souls within us, and use the help of the Divine or Universe (whichever you prefer) to walk the paths ahead of us, that have, trust me, already been preordained.

We can maintain healthy spirituality, by taking care of our minds and bodies, and also our auras (which are basically our external energy shields). By doing that, our spirits are taken care of. The essence of being, and the birthplace of thought, action or deed is our spirit. We must keep it free and unhinged.

This book is a testament to that fact, on how to keep your spirit unhinged, and unabashedly enjoy the beauties and pleasures of life. For that is the purpose of life, which has been given to us only once!

We all have a soul mission, and we must carry it out. And just like walking on a path, sometimes we must stop to smell the roses…

And those roses are poetry, they are music, they are theatre, are art, are anything and everything beautiful that the mind can conceive.

PREFACE

This life is about celebrating the beauty of all the aspects of life. Just like we should face failure with a determined brow, we must equally face happiness with laughter. Nothing must faze us; after all, it's a journey, and there will be rocks on the road. While walking this path, sometimes we will get hurt, and sometimes we will see a great scenery, say the majestic vision of the orange sun setting in the horizon!

For what is crooked, must also be straightened. Your life will never be a collection of only roses or only thorns but a generous mix of both. That's why you should learn to hurt as much as to feel pleasure. Smile or cry, both are human.

I hope and wish each and every reader of this book appreciates it for the purpose of writing the book. Which is to connect with my readers on a soul-level. And to write poetry that plays with their heart-strings. I am more a violinist than a poet, actually, if you may believe that. My job is to lure you into a world of our own, yours and mine, where I make you sit, and paint for you great visions that will surely astound you! Then with the subtle music of the rolling letters, as in my poetry, I will try to sing to you a ballad that you will carry deep-beneath yourself, probably in your soul.

So, abound this great adventure, and prepare to get rocked and moved!

1. A dance with the Bloody Mary

Clouds dismantled,
And Angels were born,
A bloody rose, with a single,
Silver thorn…

Talk of the town was on their lips,
How she danced with the Devil,
How she shook her hips…

She dropped roseate petals,
As she moved,
Her thorns,
Kept the people grouped…

Night dawned,
As they all fawned,
On her…

The Devil, as an empowerment,
Took his leave…

The woman,
Left hopes and thoughts,
To bereave.

When the lights went out,
There was a maniacal laughter,
The people were petrified,
What would happen after?

Swiftly and with grace,
She took each of them
By the face,
And sunk her hellish teeth,
To their grimace…

The She-Devil,
On her run,
A lucky streak,
A child of nature,
A freak!

On their blood,
She feasted her soul…

As their souls,
Made her whole!

Drat to love,
Drat to romance,
Drat to marriage,
Drat to perchance…

A woman who knows,
How to make her whole,
A hellish feast,
Of blood and soul…

And as the night whispered away,
Its smoky mist,
The barroom woke up to a
Sunny feast.

Lifeless bodies,
Strewn like hay,
One would wonder,
Will the cattle come to prey?

And as the morning,
Wore its majestic robe,
The scene came to a finale,
Like a longing probe…

Desire and temptation,
Forever be,
Dance with the Bloody Mary,
You will never forget,
She…

2. A December so cold

The winter swings lie empty,
Rocking to the sweet, dark melody
Of Pride, Spoilt Lipstick, Dank Whiskey,
And everything in between…

God knows, he played games here,
So…

The deaf moon, breathes Her last,
Sighing symphony into the breezeless wind,
That rocks the swings,
Atleast, in my eyes…

She said, she would come,
She said she would,
And hence I waited…
And hence I disregarded the entire World,
And hence, I waited…

Now the evening crashes upon,
My unborn heart,
Beating it black and purple.

The blood burns in the pyre,
Of funerals of more…

The nightling creeps silently,
Traveling through Time and Hyperspace,
Frantically,
To make Us meet.

But death pays a Toll,
And the Satan laughs
As he rolls...

Dreams and expectations,
A Decade old,
Burns in the funeral pyre,
Of a December so cold...

Heavens,
Send her a letter,
Carrying my name,
And my face,
Decorated by flowers and leaves,
Tell her to find me,
Tell her to make me hers...
Tell her where I am,
With the wind that murmurs...

Tell her I am waiting,
Tell her time is sparse,
Tell her I am looking for her,
In spiritual meets,
And lonely bars...

And after she's done,
Let me know the fateful place,
To Hell with society,
To Hell with disgrace.

For if not December,
Then January would definitely
Find a place…
For two lovers in this cruel world,
For the two of them to embrace…

3. A harmony in fifth

The joyous shout of the mariner,
A prosperous mariner,
Rolled like golden coins,
Soothing his voice,
Over the din…

A man of great wealth,
And wisdom…
A well travelled man,
A man of great renown…

Who wouldn't desire such a man?

And the most darling woman,
In town,
Fell for his crown…
His suave and charming ways…

Eyes like a doe,
Skin of porcelain, so clear
That you can trace your
Future on it.

Limousines, and grand gestures,
Filled her days,
Gifts from the Mariner…

A man of great wealth and wisdom.

Who knows?
If someday she wants,
He may even buy her the moon…

Expensive galas,
And opulent balls,
All in the chambers of his
Royal mansions…

Wealth so abundant,
That the point isn't money anymore,
It is the comfort and freedom,
It buys…

If love were a plaything,
It wouldn't bother these two…

For they were truly,
In love.

His childhood dreams,
Things only money can buy,
Were as easy to get,
As anything…

The magnificent mornings,
The opulent afternoons,
And the grand evenings,
Leading to,
Intense and romantic nights…

Who wouldn't want this man?

Certainly not this darling natured
Good hearted,
Loyal woman, of great beauty,
Who was the absolute
Apple-of-the-eye
Of his.

This 40 something man,
Had a ring to his voice,
Like a thousand gold coins,
Rolling down a pebbled road…
His faith and his gratitude,
His behaviour showed…

And the admiration for that,
In her eyes, glowed!

4. A manual to surviving a heartbreak

Yes,
You have loved…
And you have loved
Deeply, soulfully, even if a bit
Longingly.

Yes,
You have felt your doubt
Separate, the hollows between
Surety, and doubt,
And alchemize itself,
To Great Faith…

A place on Earth,
Where there is no
Skepticism,
Or doubt,
A place,
Where love flows freely,
And is given away like
Petrichor,
Before the thundering rain…
Freely,
And surely,
With consequence…

And yes,
They have left…

They have lied and cheated…

They have betrayed,
Without thinking once of your
Great,
Undivided,
True,
Love…

It confounds you
How it could happen?

How can a sane person,
Abandon your Love?
A Love that was true and faithful?
A love that was fulfilling
And nourishing?
A love that made life
Seem bearable?
And a little more,
Liveable?

But,
Knock knock,
They have left...
They have left the cinders of
Broken, seethed love,
At their wake...
In this fire,
They have burnt,
Your heart and soul,
Your truth and your whole...

But, fret not,
This fire,
That now seems to engulf you...
Something you want to
Escape so desperately?
A fire, and storm
That puts you in despair...

My brave child,
Bite your lips,
And brave it...

For this fire shall die,
And this storm will pass,
The love letters you have collected,
Will collect rust,
Their memories will fade,
And Spring will call,
Bright flowers will bloom,
And sweet birds will chirp...

And they will no longer be there...
In your heart and soul and minds...

You will be freed,
From a love that was poison,
That not even the vilest of snakes,
Can produce...

And the fire would have purged you,
You will become a Phoenix...

The hailing storm,
With its cobbled stones,
Bruised you black, and blue...

A soul of steel, my child,
You have made,
Where no hail or storm,
Or cobbled stones,
Can bruise...

My child,
This broken heart,
Will make you a Superman!

And those that have left,
Will want to come back,
To experience your newfound
Strength…
But your radiance,
And positivity,
Will scare them away!

This bad love,
Will make space for,
A love that is destined,
And fated.
A love that,
Does not look down upon
Someone whose feelings
Have been manipulated.
A love that is sure to stay,
A love that will make you say…
"I am grateful to have loved!"

Just don't lose hope!

5. A separation

It started out as,
A gift from Spring,
A cherished entanglement,
Which rode through,
Summer, Autumn and Winter.

Both were waiting for signs,
And then the love appeared,
A love so fine…

Having crossed the steeple,
And in the midst of a thousand people,
Who had come to shout and cheer,
The old, appreciated their courage,
Sheer.
The sun was still shining…

Missed calls,
Tight deadlines,
Work on the weekends…
They both wondered,
How to spend more time,
With each other.

And as the days passed,
The hours of hearty conversation,
Trickled down to a monosyllable.

Days,
Went by,
Without love,
Or conversation…

Then they started building walls,
Against each other,
A love so fine,
That in the summer sun,
Did shine,
Now lay like a rusty nail,
On the coffin,
Of their failed romance…

It took,
One paper,
Two signatures,
And a heartful of tears,
And regrets,
And painful separation,
And convincing themselves,
To be without each other.

A Spring's breeze,
Brought them together,
A winter's chill,
A cold, dank eventuality,
One legal paper,
And they were
Divorced.

6. A wise man

A wise man,
And an Enlightened man,
Will see,
Life as it is…

It is not a superpower,
Instead it is the mind,
Overcoming the mythical Karmic Cycle,
Break free of the basket,
That blinds our heads.

A regular person,
Will see a thing for what is shown,
And Me?
I see everything as it is,
In every precept of Time,
Where Time itself is absent,
And an illusion…
Mortality exists in a plane,
Without the countable existence of
Time, or other measures.

People complain about corruption,
And disease,
And infamy…
To my eyes,
They are all eventualities.

As Human Beings,
We are building the World,
Based on our choices,
From among our options.

And the world is like a Kaleidoscope,
Everyone's actions jut in,
To create an aggregate reality!

There is no such thing as
Sin or virtue,
The soul knows an Energy,
That is healthy for it.
And each action,
That demeans the soul,
That Humanity has been scared of,
And hence named Sin.

We live by false precepts,
Of Justice and Law and Order,
They are just like,
Rearing Cattle,
Like a shepherd dog,
Keeping people from falling over
The edge,
Preventing Hatred...

But only as a token,
Real Hatred,
Exists in people's Hearts...
And that cannot be changed,
Unless the individual,
Has realized,
That no amount of hatred or malice,
Can punish or bring Justice to them,
Without them burning first.

This world was not meant for fairness,
And justice.
They are Human concepts.
This world exists for us Humans,
As just a sandbox for our actions,
Which too,
Despite to our much agony,
Predetermined to a certain extent...

We Seek something,

God or love or whatever,
Thinking our virtues will reward us…
It is an Outlaw's world,
Those who reach out and grab
What they want,
Only they will win…

And to hide these from Humanity,
Oh Lord,
A million, countless stories have been told,
And minds befuddled by false morality,
And values.

In the end we seek something we cannot get,
And even if we get it,
Our fears and insecurities,
Will take them away from us again…

They say false "Adages" like
Nothing lasts forever…

If you eject yourself out of the system,
That causes you to lose the things you have,
You can make things last forever…

The fear of losing causes you to hide your
Victories, and loved things,
And the more you hide,
The more the wolves of the society,

Will hound you!

So just be functional,
And lose the illusion,
There is no God,
But there is Energy,
You can summon it,
And you can bend it
To your will…

Be that courageous fuck,
Who doesn't let time
Or eventuality control their lives…

Be that fuck,
And change your life,
After having owned it…

7. A woman of substance

A woman of substance,
Where is she?

Someone who stands up for herself,
Despite the society,
And sticks to what she believes in,
Despite criticism and stigma?

Where is she,
A woman who refuses to be
Bogged down by the weight
Of sardonicism or judgement.

Where is that woman,
Who would stand up for her love,
And follow it,
All the way through?

Where is she?
Who is unafraid,
To take a risk,
And run amock,
With her heart?

Where is she?
Who doesn't look for wealth,
Other than her own…

Where is she?
Who can fight for her man,
Till her dying breath,
And have her man,
Doing the same?

Who dares love so,
Love a man,
Who society judges,
But cannot slip,
From the pages of her heart.

The woman,
Who would stand up for herself,
Despite difficulties,
And not choose the easy way out,
By conforming…

Where is she?

8. Africa

I wanna go to Africa,
Again.
I wanna immerse myself,
In the simple rustic beauties,
Of African daily lives.

I wanna melange in the yellows,
And the purples,
And the myriad hues,
Of African sunsets,
In the bush.

I want to be friends,
With African women,
Strong, sturdy with an
Ample frame…

Their slight mockeries,
Their unapologetic
Flirtations,
Strong women are found here…

And then I wanna kiss Lions,
On a Safari, too!

The electric atmosphere,
Tempered by the solace
Of the African Savannas,
Call to me!

Retro TV's,
And a beer called Tusker,
There's a bee and a busker,
On the streets of Nairobi.

The vast expanse of African grasslands,
Makes you feel small…

A thousand miles away the sun sets,
Like burning rum on orange juice…

The sunset belongs to no one,
As doesn't anything else.
You have come to feel and touch,
Leave only your footprints…

9. Believer

And you think I am a plain-Joe.

But have you been with me,
In my head?
Have you heard me speaking
Passionately,
About my dreams,
And lofty goals?

Have you been with me long
Enough,
For me to turn you into a
Believer?

10. Drugs

Don't drop shit,
Drop funk,
Lounge with a cigarette,
Like a funky monk.

Horatio,
Ain't a nice guy,
Too cool to be true,
He don't give no fuck,
Oh, he is so fly!

Sugar and spice,
Baby, I'm dying in the ice…

Loafers fill the avenue,
The government counts
The revenues.
Lollypops and candy floss,
Gaussian,
Like a bloody Faust.

Knowledge is power,
Sex for hire,
Education to the toots,
Baby, look at me,
I am the loots.

A dystopia of epic proportions,
A slight disarray of emotions,
We should all be learning the lessons,
Of a public ramshackle…

Hold on tight,
While I fly you,
To the moon so white…
Eager bone,
The bloody moon shone,
Babe,
That's an ice-cream cone…

Social anarchy,
Seasoned with chaos,
My pussycat,
You love her meows!

Coasting along,
Like a fine yacht,
That bloody lad,
Is an inch short,
Of Hell,
I tell you…

He snort,
Like the coke don't
Give up,
Fancy or dream,
Coke, or Malana cream?

After trashing the entire humanity,
Dousing in profanity,
The cunt wants some clarity,
Marry me…

Lover's lores,
Sold like bloody whores,
Books of pages,
Relationships of cages.

The mind wanders free,
Wondering if she'd choose me!
Horatio Nelson,
And Mel Gibson…

They both look for a scene,
Laced with coke and codeine…

This drug song,
Has no end,
Riding risky,
Braving the bends,
In my fast car,
Looking for the next bar…

Peace.

11. Father

Father,
You are the Sun of my life.
Despite all the setbacks,
And the difficulties,
I gave you.
You never gave up,
On your hope,
To turn me into a good man,
Out.

The man that you are,
Inspires and motivates me.

You have always been an example,
Inspiring me to move,
With confidence,
And overcome my failures.

You taught me courage,
In the face of adversity.

You brought me up with want,
So that later I could attain,
What I want,
With the right mindset.

You were strong as rock,
Never yielding under pressure…
And God knows,
I gave you enough to worry about!

You made me a rock-hard man,
Deflecting all of the miseries,
That overcame me.

You made me so strong,
That now you rely on me,
For the protection of the family…
And I am only too happy to comply.

You taught me to be Honest and Faithful,
Now I am a straight man,
And that absolutely came out of your fan.

Thank you for raising me right,
Thank you…

12. Hurtful Heaven

The alcohol lingers,
On my lips.
The dark smoke of the smoky alley,
Shows me its hips.
This city is a dystopian pleasure-pot,
Not the balmy heaven,
That I had thought.

I never knew people were this way,
One thing they mean, another thing they say…
I didn't know people were so hateful,
And vile, and Godless…
I never knew you were so heartless.

Our love is over, and the times
Have been remembered,
Like engraving on tree trunks,
Like familiar mantra chanted by monks…

Our world was a Heaven,
In which resided only You and I.
The clouds diffracted a Heavenly color,
And everything was so sublime!

But woe it be!
You couldn't be mine…

Now my world has been torn apart,
I have to start from the start,
And though I let you go,
I keep a piece of you,
In my heart…

13. My Kosen Rufu Partner

It really titillates the Soul,
To tell you, I love you,
Like this.
In secrecy,
Sitting in my room…

No, I will not say your name,
Because a million and one,
Eyes are watching.
And I would really like this thing
To happen.

But you know who you are,
Sweet co-practitioner.

I would really like to be your
Kosen-Rufu partner.
Hold your hand,
And heal the infamies of
The world.

Through our light,
We shall dispel ignorance
And malady.

Your soft, delicate touch,
And my determined hands,
Together we will build this World,
For a better tomorrow.

I have started out,
In this life,
It's been a year now…

Had been chasing a Master's Degree,
And the glory and honour that
Comes with it.

Sadly,
That couldn't happen…
Probably,
Because I had to meet you!
At the Kaikan!

I have been all over the world,
And even fell in love once or twice,
But none of that were ever True.
And the Gohonzon didn't let it happen…

But you I am sure of.
Because when we met,
I asked Gohonzon,
Whether you were the One,
And he very assuredly said, yes,
You, you know who you are,
You are the One.

I recognised you at first sight,
You seemed familiar.
In a whole room full of people,
You were glowing like a Lamp!

It was immediately clear to me,
That you were mine…
And since then,
Instead of wasting time on
Being a fool, by being Romantic
Out of the way;
I have been spending each waking hour
Developing myself,
And creating something solid,
For us to go by…

Would you please,
Hold my hand?
And we will cross oceans
Together.
And bring the World closer,
A little at a time?

I love you…

14. My own spring

The love, in divine roses,
The mirth in dancing posies,
The wind, like a cashmere shawl,
God's answer to summer and fall…

The sweet honey that bees make,
The lemonade you forgot to make,
The zest that the atmosphere bakes,
The sorrow, the calumny,
That the Spring takes…

Balmy winds, and serene scenes,
A pop in your gait,
The curious tale of one's fate,
The fight between bad and good,
Spring takes it all,
It should.

Ballerinas cascading like water,
A stream, a waterfall,
A child of nature,
Spring's daughter…

The abundant smiles,
And the beaming faces,
The benevolent wind,
Leaves kaleidoscope traces…

The pattern of beauty,
Love and laughter,
We enjoy in this life,
And take it to the
Everafter.

A stony bridge,
A lonely island,
We speak with our cloudy dreams,
The night remains,
Silent.

A crazy lark,
Hovering in the sky,
The beauty of Spring,
Doth make me cry…

Speaking in tunes,
Beneath the roving moon,
Talks of love,
Like tufty clouds,
Or cotton candy,
Spring's charm was warm and
Dandy.

The evening breeze,
Blows without permission,
Easing the gall,
Of our days,
Ending the work day,
With grace.

The coconut trees,
Sway their assent,
Spring has come,
With the Heaven's descent,
Of all things beautiful,
Caught in limbo…

Fairytales and fireflies,
Dancing petunias,
And butterflies,
The freshest blooms,
Smelling divine,
This spring,
I call it mine…

15. Remembrance

I have lived,
On and on,
In ages,
In times,
Far from now…

I remember the pristine
Tranquil nights,
The open and free
Laughter.

I remember the ethereal
Sky,
That cast a magic spell
On all.

The sunlight was balmy,
And smooth,
And loving,
One's heart,
It did soothe.

And there were elephants,
And there were horses,
All the King's men,
Went by,
Through their daily courses.

I have loved,
A love so deep,
That even time froze,
To document it.
Time arose,
To exemplify it,
Over the ages.

And that is what people swear by…

Oh dear friend,
Oh dear, dear
Hold me in thy fragile grips,
I'll make my getaway,
And search for the Sun.

As I have, over the ages, and over lifetimes

Along with you

16. Rules

People making rules,
All the time,
About everything.

Tell me, dear fellow,
Before you crafted these rules,
Were there any rules to begin with?

You said,
The day is 24 hours.
When dinosaurs roamed the Earth,
Did they know of 9 PM,
A sacred hour for dinner?

You said,
You cannot stop loving a person.
Tell me,
Have you ever loved so deeply,
Hurt so badly,
That the thought of living
Feels like punishment?

Not so savory now, is it?

You said,
Eyes don't lie.
But I've seen sinners—
Countless sinners—
Lie with their eyes,
All the time.

You said,
True love waits.
Oh, brother of mine,
Nothing waits.
Time is fluid;
It flows and carries
Everything away.

I tried waiting.
I tried loving.
I even tried having dinner at 9.

But life became clearer,
Sharper,
When I realized—
This fleeting time I hold
Is far too precious
For your
Goddamn rules.

17. She would turn to me

The only emotion I feel
Is loneliness.
And yes, pain…
Although pain is not an emotion.

This rote life spins,
Circles upon circles.
Nothing has changed;
I still haven't found my person.

(Or even if I have, she is not mine, yet.)
I've just seen her,
Like a bird in a tree,
Perched at a distance,
Never close.

Oh, how I wish
She would talk to me.
How I wish
We could share moments,
Her hands in mine,
Walking this Earth,
Forever.

But she prefers silence,
And I am left with whispers
Of what could be.

18. The Dazzling Demise of La

The shrill pines, the covenant,
So blind,
Like the thin, screeching scream,
Of the dying pigs…

Like wind they blow through,
The corridors,
Where life and death dance,
Like nude lovers.

Slaughterhouse,
Of pigs,
We need one,
For the bigwigs…

Rosy red,
Wine,
And shred…

The thin flowers cry,
The fat ones,
Desecrate,
The names of
Raphael and Michaelangelo…

Creators,
Laid in dust.

The little Mormons,
Can't control their
Hormones,
They protest,
The death of a butterfly,
And forget about the
Life,
Of the beggar.

Screams unite,
Countries of the world,
The agents of infamy,
Sells their worth
In gold.

Rampage,
In heaven,
Sins, absolucy,
Sire,
There are seven…

Hence arises,
The saviour,
But arise,
Is all he does,
For who listens to
God
Anymore?

19. The Dictator

The oppressive shackles,
Pull me back, like a rubber band,
The fool, traversing like a bird,
On skies of grey and melange.

The collective rises to a whole,
We punish the man with a hole,
In his shirt.
The man, who got the whole,
From a successful bullet,
In an unsuccessful rebellion,
Of the powerful and the weak,
The rich and the poor,
The jealous and the meek.

Red, is the colour of the setting sun,
Red is the color of the ruddy cheek,
Which took the blow, of opposition,
Of Good and the Geek.

Bloody streams run down the broadways
Of malice,
Little children have been planted here...

And one summer day,
Primroses will bloom,
In the graves of those distant and near.

The whole world died at your feet,
You tyrant,
You make your drum beat,
You make them skies carry the news,
Of infamy, and cholera and soul abuse.

Your solo' dolo',
Dancing like a Papa Pancho,
Brother you can't swallow your damn
Nacho…

Which you borrowed…
Borrowed? Stole!

Today the castles have rumbled,
And the sleepers have shifted,
In their beds…

Blooming roses have sacrificed their reds…

The color of blood now paints the green…
Stock markets and bitcoins,
They celebrate your win.

You are a Lion,
Yes you are!
But as a lion,
You are a Monster!

• 54 •

Be careful!
For the world seethes so!
What happened once,
Can again happen,
Moreso…
People of the world unite,
And the throne beneath your back,
Will move,
Your bloody carcass,
On the rack of tyrants,
Will sail for the bloody moon.

20. The Finish Line

The slight serenade,
Like the cascade,
Of a waterfall,
Save played by lonely melody,
Of shimmery golden threads,
Of the blinds of your room;
The slight shrill chime…

The slight attack,
Of the heart,
By the knife of your love…
Scars me in such,
Pleasurable pain.

Your dark eyes,
Are the panacea to my
Hurt, and misery…

And after you have taken
My heart,
Don't turn it to Art…
Turn it into,
A fresco,
A staunch rock,
Which an ocean of Time,
Shall kiss and smooch,
In the vagaries of our Destinies.

You have started,
And so have I…

Decorating your nubile body,
By wreaths of flowers,
Everyday,
Baby, it's just a mile to the finish…

Envelop me, and consume me,
Meet me at the finish line.
Meet me there in good time,
With a laugh, a hug,
And a victory shared only
With mine.

We shall dance our lives away,
Far from the fray,
And the madding crowds…

21. The first flush of moonlight

The silvery moonlight,
The gush of a first sight,
The melody of love,
Sweet and mellow…

A love that isn't shallow,
A sweet I'll wholly swallow,
A bit of peace,
That is only mine…

Her eyes like a whisper,
Beckon and bicker,
The moonlight shines upon
Her eyelashes…

And love gushes forward,
God, I am such a coward!
I watch her like,
A child watches a sparrow…

In trees, or dreamy whispers,
A dog with his whiskers,
Oh Lord, how I'd love to,
Lean in and kiss her…
Her rosy cheeks blush,
And her porcelain skin glows,
Oh God, may the right way
This path show!

Her careless banter,
Her elitist accent,
The moon styles herself,
As a crescent,
In her interstellar hair…

And I would love you babe,
More than what you crave,
I would love you,
And you would care…

22. The mountains in Bengal

The journey from the plains to the hills, is fraught with wonder and amazement. For if you are an ordinary person, the road will drag your soul by the heart, and like a dynamite, explode it all around the skirts of the road.

The gentle wind, in your ears will feel like a flute played by some herdsman in the past. The fog and the clouds, with their gentle demeanour will prepare you for the majesty that is The Kanchendzonga. The clouds teach us patience, the clouds teach us that true Love is slow.

The evening gathers around the corner of her eyes, like the Kohl on it, it gathers a certain dark energy that shocks the positivity in you, and Old Monk and Coke go well with the gathering darkness. The ethereal, dusky, velvet skies put a charm on you, one that imbibes in you, and you wonder under the stars, exactly how huge is this life in the microcosm of reality. And just like the Cheshire Cat, Divinity and Spiritual realization peeks out of the clouds, and slowly grimacing under the weight of disbelief disappears and leaves you wondering…

Nighttime falls, and all ye faithful and cold, are sleeping in their bunks. The moon dons the hat of a protector, until nighttime, until day… Then another cold morning arrives.

23. The panacea of dark times

It is a life of service,
And compassion,
A life of learning profound,
Lessons.

It is a life to give a lot,
And take little,
Expect even less.
It is a life, where the soul blooms,
Whether in mud or a garden,
Regardless.

It is a life of leading,
And guiding,
A life of healing,
And laughing.
A life of giving so much,
And taking so little,
A life of breaking prejudice,
As in their nature,
They are brittle...

Leading blind men,
Forging them in steel,
Showing them a light,
Being their keel.

A spotlight of clarity,
And good intentions,
Resisting the urge of personal gain,
And honorary mentions.

In an age of such darkness,
In such an age,
Bringing light to the populace,
Resisting temptation and desire,
Purging souls in the eternal fire.

Judging,
Not for the sake of judgement,
But for the good of mankind,
For the highest upliftment of
Public good.
I know what I must do,
I know, what I should!

Jails and asylums,
Don't make good men.
It is the alchemic fire,
The fire of justice,
That purges a soul,
Free of all sins…

Thus burn all must,
Cleanse their souls,
After all,
Humanity must win.

This precious age of corruption
And darkness,
Is the very panacea for
For great progress.
For a thing that has never been black,
Cannot shine like a diamond
In a hay stack.

For where there is darkness,
There is light,
For where there is corruption,
Humans must fight.

And this is the age of great
Awakening, and redemption,
It is when,
My dream will find completion…

24. The Samba Stormer

Darling woman,
You dance like the wind,
Storming the Calypso moon…
Your senses set ablaze,
By the reckless Samba…

A passionate jig,
A smoldering gaze,
You bite your lips,
As it sets the floor ablaze…

Dancing like the dark storm,
Tap, tap, tap,
Your motion moves the crowd
Bereft of all norms…

The whirlwind of emotions,
That play in my mind,
Darling dancing woman,
You dance, as you leave
Propriety behind.

Each step like a firebrand,
Burns across the stage,
The appreciative crowd stands by,
Sweet lady you are a rage!

And as the dance comes to a close,
Like a sweating rose,
You flay your limbs,
So gracefully,
With the finality of
Church hymns...

And this rascal heart,
I devote to thee,
Burning you with my stare,
Waiting...
When can I hold you in my arms,
Naked and bare...

25. This beautiful Universe

I don't feel a being anymore…
I don't feel a sense of belonging,
I do not idolise this soul separation,
Just worship this consciousness.

The paradox of consciousness is,
It doesn't exist, itself.
Yet it imagines everything around it
To be true…

There is no soul centre,
We are not governed by a plan…
There is no great manuscript,
Or a Masterplan…

There is only the great conglomeration
Of energies…
Which births the colours to our visions…
It births the illusion,
That we see around ourselves…

The Universe,
Or whatever we comprehend,
Beyond comprehension,
Is just like a ball of malleable fire…
It is changing shape,
And form,
And back again…

There is no point to this,
Even to existence.
There is no reason why,
The Universe is like this,
Pointless…

It just exists in our minds…

If there were a greater truth,
A truth comprising the illusion
Of all our beings…
If there were a function for our illusions,
A job, or task,
It would make the Universe,
Understandable,
And decipherable.

If I had to minimise the cause
Of existence of the Universe
And the mankind,
I would say,
The Universe is a great garden
Of malleable energy,
And we are its flowers!

The Universe exists,
Because of everything that exists
Within it.
We are the building blocks
Of the Universe...

And I bet,
If there is a Higher Power,
That views the Universe as it is,
That Man or Woman,
Will be God...

And what will They see?
In this twisted, rickety Universe?

A cosmic Souvenir,
Of great, fragile beauty...

26. This Holi

This Holi has coloured me,
Orange.
This Holi has left me bereft
Of warmth, and exuberance.
This Holi,
I spent alone...

As I grow,
And I count my days,
I see two thing slipping off my fingers,
One, are friends,
And the other are black hair on my head...

Maybe the greying of hair, is a sign of
Wisdom.
But the lack of friends,
Is the lack of places, where I can
Apply that wisdom...

I used to trust like a fan,
Open-close.
Now, it's more complicated…
Trust,
Comes after a point of time,
We burn together…
And the purpose of burning,
Is to be smelted together.

So many women,
Like the spoils of struggle,
But will not burn with the man,
Ready made,
Like trousers,
They think,
Are love, family and career…

They are wrong…

Isolation is fun,
No expectations,
No competition,
No comparisons,
No grief…

But a point comes,
When you take so little from the World, that,
Your insides become hollow,
No sap,
Just a fun little Buddha,
Who can help,
If people are even aware,
That he exists,
And He can help…

I feel I am wasting my time
In this solitude of mine…

I have become something, I cannot explain,
I don't feel grief, happiness, joy
Or anything at all!
Life passes by without touching me…

I don't feel love, as in the traditional sense of love.
I feel a deep fatherly concern,
I feel to protect,
I feel to defend,
I feel to nurture and provide…

There are a few wrongs in my life,
That I have to right...
No vengeance, just Shifts...
I will shift my perspective from a hateful
Need of Justice,
To a peaceful vessel of love...
Who has forgiven all enemies,
All sabotageurs,
And those who pain me daily...

For them I shall pray,
For their light I shall chant,
May they abandon their
Cruel devices, and ways...

So much time,
I have spent,
On things, abstract, which do not
Attract much people...
They are the keystones to living a life,
Completely under your control,
Like in "Manual" mode...

Most people,
They like readymade,
Spirituality,
Love,
Marriage,
Careers...

They will master one art though,
That of slavishly surviving the hollow halls,
Of the corporate.

And they will earn,
And they will spend!

Today not a man or a woman,
Can paint a picture,
But they can buy burly paintings
From galleries,
Sitting on their walls,
Appreciated only when the guests arrive…

They know what they want,
And they know where they can buy it…

Phooey to hobbies and passions,
We can buy everything now!

This is the royal submission to the great
Machine!
The Machine is one which works using
The hearts, hardwork and souls of
Human Beings.
It is a non-living yet living construct,
It is feeding on us…

It is in our minds, and in our bodies,

It is in our souls and daily lives.

It exists to exist.

And we exist to feed it...

27. Time is lying in the sunshine

When I was down,
Many people put on a
Frown…
Stylised by pretense,
And beautified by
A hatred for me,
My very being.

It was like a bird
Had dropped on
The ground,
And now it must
Be killed,
For it is not
Flying.
Rendering it,
Weak,
And vulnerable.

Consider God,
If He fell,
People will reduce Him,
And try to take his place.
Oh Joy!

Anyone who holds a coveted,
Seat,
Has to watch his ass,
Or pay by the beats…

And those unaware,
Children mostly,
The Chosen Ones,
People who shine in everything…
Conspiracies are their,
Redemption.
A price for being so good,
To have the audacity
Of being Extraordinary…

The sweet lullaby
Of the clock ticking,
That's the windmill of time…

Your time has come.

28. Wise women

Every woman has complained about,
Men...

That they are unfaithful,
Dishonest,
Roving eyes,
Unmodest.

But, but,
My dear friend,
When a man of good character,
And nature,
Does perchance visit them,
In their lives...

What do they do?

They instantly disbelieve him,
And stigmatise him,
Considering the crimes done to women,
By Mankind.

And lo' behold,
When such a man comes,
The revenge switch,
Gets triggered in a woman's brains…

First,
She will subject him to
The torture she has received,
From other men…

And when that is done,
She will torture him,
For the torture received by
Other women she knows.

And finally,
She will torture him,
For just being a man…

And when she's done,
And the man is broke
In all ways;
She will say,
Oh such a loser,
And lose him to the fray…

Women,
I thought were wise…

29. You are everything

Why?
Why do I give it my all
Everytime,
To be met with,
Disappointment and heartbreak,
Everytime?

I seek the forbidden fruit,
Of the apple tree,
So innocuous,
Such that Human beings,
Won't find it…

It seems like vultures are,
Encircling that lignite structure,
There's so much path left,
For me to tread,
And trudge…

The sunlight burns my heart,
The ephemeral smoke that arises,
Laughs maniacally,
And makes its way to the
Coffers,
Of heavenly sacrifices…

The disappointments,
And failures…
Rejections and rebuttals,
Lie like dead cigarettes,
On the grounds,
Left by some irresponsible,
Punk.

The great river of sorrow,
Flows through my heart,
Occasionally sniggering,
At my bent and broken,
Mechanisms.

Loving allurements,
Turn into,
Snarky chidings,
Ripping open my heart.

The daylight speaks,
As the sky rends open,
Its heart,
By its most favourite,
Lightning bolt,
Descended upon the Earth,
From the Vajradanda of
Indra.

The daylight speaks,
It teaches me to count,
And taste,
The pickles that my grandma
Lay in the sun.
To rot...

But, the sky shows me,
That the rotting pickles taste
Better, than the original fruit.

Maybe my heart,
Is like a pickle.
It may taste better,
Or sour,
But experience surely
Has defeated the ashes
Of the cemetery...

I learn my own company,
It is more fulfilling than,
The fake, hollow promises
Of a lover,
Who is a bloody Pretender!

The tallest building in this
Town,
Teaches me grace and self respect.
The dying sunlight,
Kisses my eyes,
Promising me,
A life that is simple and bereft
Of sin.

A life without love?

I wonder.

And then,
The bluest peacock
Comes into my mind,
And says,
You are Everything!

30. Poverty

Hello Monsieur,
Fancy seeing you here,
This part of town...
Neon lights,
*Red lights,
Beautiful women,
*Prostitutes.
Welcome to the Dump.

You can hear screams,
They aren't coming from churches,
They are people getting stabbed,
Choked, cloaked, killed...
*Real life.

Life gets real here,
You better park your Jag
In the next block.
For I'm sure you'll be missing
A tire,
After 15 minutes.

Fancy some Crack?
*Crack cocaine, narcotics.
Illegal shit.

Ideology, you embody, is
Something you make movies,
Books, and music out of.
The only music I hear, Sire
Is the Police Sirens,
*911, what's your emergency?

You have come to indulge,
I have come to divulge,
My heart full of hatred,
And black.
*Cardiac arrest, stat. stat. stat.

I was promised dinner,
Here,
By that cardboard box regiment.
Throwaway chicken nuggets,
*Beluga Caviar, at the Ritz
Some stale bread,
*Smoked Salmon,
A little hooch,
*Moet-et-Chandon, get your dance on.

Welcome, and goodbye,
Poverty doesn't suit you…

www.ingramcontent.com/pod-product-compliance
Lightning Source LLC
Chambersburg PA
CBHW040826120726
48005CB00012B/1514